A CxO Handbook to
Blockchain

By

Rajan Kashyap

ISBN: 978-0-244-78220-7

PublishNation
www.publishnation.co.uk

Introduction

Blockchain has been making a lot of headlines in the last couple of years. There is, however, a lot of confusion around the use of the technology. Sometimes it feels like it is a solution looking for a problem. Most of the people only think that it is bitcoin. Some organisations want to use the technology but is not sure where to start.

This book will provide the knowledge of the technologies, how and where it fits, how are the industries using it and how to start on the journey.

I have written this book based on my numerous discussions with senior management of many diverse organisations, my experience of implementing blockchain projects and many points of view that I have built with my team.

-Author

Contents

Chapter 1 - History of Blockchain

Technology rules the world and it influences almost everything when a new one comes into existence. Take Smartphone, before its advancement, the world had simple mobile phones which were used only for talking and sending text messages to our nearest and dearest. In today's world people do everything from calling to accessing information and placing an order for the required product/service on a Smartphone.

The technology which is making news headlines day by day is known as blockchain or Block Chain. So what is a blockchain? Simply put, it is an append only shared ledger maintained by a network of computers. No single computer has control over the ledger, and a record is added to the ledger only after a common consensus. Moreover, every participating computer has an exact copy of the ledger. This ledger can contain any information, asset or transaction.

This technology did not exist in its current form until the year 2008, and it was the year 2017 when blockchain became the buzzword. It shook the entire world in almost every field, from banking and finance to manufacturing and supply chain. This technology is based on a white paper written by an author named Satoshi Nakamoto, whose identity is unknown to the world. It became the basis of the all cryptocurrencies and blockchain in general.

Bitcoin is the first known implementation of technology. In the year 2009 when bitcoin entered the market, its value was just $ 0.06. At that time very few people noticed it. Gradually, it extended its market, and its value reached $ 19,000 in December 2017. It became so famous and popular that only the term blockchain was enough to create value. To comprehend its significance here is an example:

There was a beverage selling firm, Long Island Iced Tea. The owner replaced its business name with Long Blockchain Corp. In 2017 even he knew nothing in this regard. Just after renaming the business the stock price of this beverage selling firm rose 300% in a single day.

Many companies of different sectors including banking invested in bitcoin, a very few people comprehend this technology, its source and advancement.

The Concept

In Yap, an island in the Pacific region, people used limestone to represent the value of the trade they do. It is also referred to as Rai stone and it had a hole in the middle. The stones were big, sometimes more than the size of a car, so it was not possible to carry them. However, each stone has an owner, and everyone in the community knew whom it belongs to but was rarely moved.

The ownership of the stone was changed in the presence of a minimum number of community members and was inscribed on the stone. Since inscribing on the stone was a laborious task, the person doing it, the inscriber, was given a reward in the form of the part ownership of the stone.

Since anyone could have carved a new stone and generated the currency, the supply of the stones kept increasing and the value decreasing, the currency became useless after a time.

The concept behind the development of cryptocurrency is a bit similar to a platform/system where everybody has an idea what belongs to him or her. With the use of a distributed public ledger, the cryptocurrency eliminates the need for a central authority such as a bank. At the same time, the problem of too much generation of the currency is controlled using the technique called halving.

There is a correlation between Rai Stone and cryptocurrency, i.e. bitcoin. In the current time the stone in the software form is the currency and the inscription on it is the electronic ledger. The people with faith in the system are known as nodes which are the participating computers. The community is a network of computer nodes, and everyone has a copy of the ledger. Every ledger consists of all the transactions since the inception of the currency. The inscribers, called miners, are special computer nodes.

At the time of change in the ownership, one of the parties produces the transaction with the attachment of a mathematical puzzle. The miners proceed to solve the problem and the first one to solve the puzzle claims the reward. The rest of the nodes give validation to the solution and get ready to add the held transaction to the system/chain. After the ownership transfer, all the nodes have exact transaction details.

The node that solves the puzzle first has to check the transaction validation and the balance of the initiating party. It does this using the copy of all the transactions held in the past. In the case of bitcoin, the transactions are circulated in a block every ten seconds. The ledger as a whole is a chain of blocks, leading to name, blockchain.

The Beginning

It is widely believed that blockchain has an association with Satoshi Nakamoto. However, it is hard to forget the work done by W. Scott Stornetta and Stuart Harber. It was the year 1991 when they worked on a cryptographically secured chain of blocks. They wanted to develop a system in which no one could tamper with the documents. Haber, Bayer and Stornetta succeeded in the incorporation of Markle Trees Design in 1992, and this work improved the efficiency in collecting various document certifications into one block.

The real conceptualisation of blockchain relates to the publication of a white paper: "Bitcoin – A Peer to Peer Electronic Cash System". It marked the real beginning of cryptocurrency, bitcoin. Satoshi Nakamoto, a person or a group of persons, published this white paper in 2008 and paved the way of direct online payment from one party to another without any involvement of a third party. According to this paper, it is an electronic payment system which is based on cryptographic proof in place of trust. The publication of this white paper relates to a need felt in 2007/8. In this time of sub-prime crisis, the economists felt that there would be a decentralised system to avoid the trust issues that was the cause of the entire financial crisis.

The white paper provided a solution for the issues relating to a centralised system and double spending. By nature it is easy to copy digital currency and spend it more than once. This paper solved this by linking one transaction to another in a tamper resistant manner. The manner described by Satoshi Nakamoto was the public ledger, and this enabled the network to examine every transaction history of the electronic coin that a person submits for payment. As a result a break on double spending has come into existence.

As a decentralised database, blockchain is copied on several nodes or computers. All of the nodes contain the same information. As the name suggests, the information is stored as blocks. Every block can have several transactions with a unique reference number for each. Each block is chained, using a reference, to the previous block and this chain continues till the first ever block. The reference used to chain the blocks is a cryptographic hash of the previous block. In simple words, every block can access all the prior blocks down to the first one of the chain, the genesis block. The time stamp produces an absolute sequential position to every block in the chain.

A transaction represents the way of blockchain's functions. In business dealing, the seller gets ready to sell a product/service to a customer for one coin. The buyer submits a transaction to one of the nodes telling the network that it wants to move one coin to the seller. The network decides if the transaction should be committed to the ledger or not using an already agreed consensus algorithm. The nodes in the network receive the transaction and verify that the buyer has the necessary coin balance and only then commits to the ledger. The verification process starts with having a look at the last transaction done by the buyer. Further, it makes sure that the buyer (node) has sufficient funds for making the purchase. Once a block is committed to the ledger it cannot be changed. Since the same copy of the chain is with every node, for a single node to create a fraudulent transaction is almost impossible as the other nodes will not agree to the transaction and will not add the transaction to their copy of the ledger. This whole process makes the blockchain completely transparent.

Advancement of the Blockchain Technology

In the beginning, the blockchain technology only drew the attention due to its ability to be anonymous, like in the case of cryptocurrency, bitcoin. However, the actual appeal to this technology is the transparency, tracking and immutability that it offers.

Many businesses have found that this technology is useful in an ever growing number of applications in almost all industry sectors. The real advancement of this technology started in 2013 when Ethereum introduced smart contracts. At the time of bitcoin launch,

Vitalik Buterin (the co-founder of Etherum and bitcoin magazine) was very hopeful. Later on, he got frustrated due to the programming limitations of the bitcoin. In 2015 he came up with the second public blockchain known as Ethereum. The difference between these two is that the later can record assets like loans and contracts apart from the currency. Gradually, it became popular and had drawn the attention of IT big players like Microsoft, UBS and BBVA.

Noticing the usefulness and popularity, IBM opened an innovative research centre to work on blockchain development in Singapore in July 2016. In November 2016 a group of professionals working for the World Economic Forum held a meeting and discussed what blockchain could do on the development of governance models. Research published by the Accenture states that the adoption rate of blockchain technology was 13.05% within the financial services in 2016. Also, the year 2016 saw another advancement and industry trade groups come together to develop a Global Blockchain Forum. As per a Gartner report published in May 2018, only 1% of CxOs were interested in the adoption of this technology, and 8% of CxOs had a plan to adopt it in forthcoming days. In November 2018, the European Parliament's Trade Committee backed the plan to use the blockchain technology to boost the trade.

The Applications of the Blockchain Technology

Blockchain technology has become very popular due to its most successful product, bitcoin. As a type of cryptocurrency, bitcoin works as a public ledger for all transactions done on the network. It has solved the issue of double and unauthorised spending and removed the need of the third party in any transaction. To comprehend the scope of the blockchain, here is an exciting story of Mariana told by *The Economist*. The story describes how this technology could make Mariana's life different.

Mariana Catalina Izaguirre was about to possess the official title of the land of her home in Honduras. According to the paper with the Property Institute, another person owned the land. A case was filed against her and the court ordered eviction. Mariana Catalina Izaguirre tried to prove her case but her home was gone by that time. According to *The Economist,* she would not lose her case if she had recorded her deed with blockchain. No one could have claimed the ownership of her homeland.

Consider the application of credit letters. Banks issue credit letters that serve as a payment guarantee when the customers fulfil certain conditions for taking loans. With the use of smart contracts and blockchain, the need of the third party (here a bank) in such transaction would be removed.

Gradually, this technology is moving to other fields like healthcare, manufacturing, digital advertising, cybersecurity, digital currency, supply chain management and cloud storage. Like the use of computers and the internet, it is expected that every sector would use blockchain technology in forthcoming years.

Chapter 2 – Most Common Use Cases

In the last chapter, we got a glimpse into the intricate history of blockchain from being a new kid in the Fintech industry to being the most sought after technology in all domains. Blockchain features today in leading news headlines and umpteen book titles, to conversations among the financial experts.

For most laymen blockchain is a term most associated with bitcoins and cryptocurrencies. The association is so deep for some that they refer to the cryptocurrency movement as the blockchain movement.

Taking into consideration the ubiquitous use of blockchain from healthcare to manufacturing to government office, its exclusive association with cryptocurrencies is misleading. However, there is a reason for this supposed association. The reason is that blockchain only gained prominence after bitcoin and other cryptocurrencies started thriving in the market.

The brief history which explains the association of blockchain with cryptocurrencies goes as
Satoshi Nakamoto published the first white paper of bitcoin in 2008, and users mined the first block of bitcoin in 2009. The bitcoin protocol was an open source protocol, many forked and initiated alternate versions of P2P currencies. As a result, faster and better altcoins like Ether and Litecoin emerged.

However, since 2014, investors realised that blockchain could be used in services beyond cryptocurrencies and started investing in projects that involved operations beyond P2P cryptocurrency transactions. Therefore, blockchain found a wide range of applications, from being used in sectors spanning pharma, banking, government and educational institutions to gaming and supply chain. Blockchain progressed from being a mere platform for bitcoin to being a groundbreaking technology finding use in many institutions involved in non-crypto operations.

The Emerging forms of Blockchain

Bitcoin introduced the term "blockchain" in the financial and corporate sector. As more and more digital assets used this technology, blockchain gained prominence as a platform to record transactional information in a transparent, immutable and decentralised manner.

The next milestone was the realisation that blockchain could be used for various kinds of transactions as well as agreements like P2P insurance, ride-sharing and P2P energy trading.

Thereafter, Ethereum emerged and added a new property to the blockchain, smart contracts. Addition of smart contract meant that you could make the transactions programmable and a piece of code can execute a contract term as soon as a condition is met, e.g. as soon as buyers receive the goods, smart contract transfers the agreed money to sellers' accounts and registers the transaction on blockchain.

Public Blockchains

The common feature across the platforms like bitcoin, Ethereum, and later entries like Dash and Litecoin is that these are public blockchain which means anyone can participate in the network. They are open source and allow participation of anyone with internet access without requiring permission. By downloading the code anybody can start working with a public node on their device and contribute to the consensus process for validating transactions. Hence, anyone can make transactions on the public blockchain.

Therefore, all the transactions that appear on such a network are transparent yet anonymous.

Private Blockchains

Those in need of greater privacy started developing another form of blockchain that could make the read permissions public but limited the write permissions to a group which could be a set of persons or organisations. Such a blockchain came to be known as a private blockchain.

Unlike a public blockchain not everyone on this network can validate the transactions and add the transaction to the blockchain; instead, the validation rights are offered by the central controlling group. The use cases of a private blockchain are seen in large enterprise operations like supply chain, auditing and track/trace.

Many companies like MultiChain and Monax have built their organisations on this private blockchain network. However, these blockchains lack the security features that are bestowed through the theoretic incentive processes used in public blockchain. Therefore, it creates the same security issues for the companies as occurs in a centralised system. Moreover, in spite of the cryptographic security, the actual powers are vested and in control of a central authority which defeats the original purpose with which blockchain was created for bitcoin.

Consortium Blockchains

Other than public and private, the other form of the blockchain which found widespread use is the Consortium or the Federation blockchain. The operations of such blockchains are not controlled by one authority, but rather by a group of more than one organisation/ representative individuals. All these entities come together and make a decision that benefits the network the most. Such a group of entities is known as a consortium or a federation, hence the name.

The consortium blockchain network offers the same privacy features as the private blockchain since not everybody with internet access can verify the transactions on this network. The way it works can be understood from the following example: For instance, a consortium may be made of 20 financial institutions, and each would operate as a node of the network. In each network, 15 may have to sign each block for validating the block. Therefore, unless a specific number of entities agree, the transactions won't be validated, giving greater security as well as private benefits to the network.

Similar to private blockchains, the right to write is limited to the internal group of participants, but the read permissions may be made public or limited to selected participants in a consortium blockchain. Therefore, such blockchains, being more scalable, faster and offering higher privacy, have been mainly adopted by the banking sector.

In a nutshell, till this date three major forms of blockchain have been in use, public blockchains, private blockchains and consortium/federation blockchains. Among them, public blockchains are mostly used in cryptocurrencies, whereas some private blockchains and most federation blockchains have found their use in non-crypto operations.

Non-Crypto use of Blockchains

As described in the previous section, many non-crypto related industries have started using private/federation blockchain because of their enhanced security features. Below is a brief description of the industries which use blockchains for operations beyond cryptocurrencies.

Finance

- **Banks**

It's ironic that the very institution which blockchain was striving to circumvent is starting to use this decentralised technology, that too at a rapid pace. As per an IBM survey, 15% of the global banks had accepted to roll out commercial and full-scale blockchain solutions. The areas where blockchain has the most significant use in banking are wholesale payments, clearing, settlement, debt issuance and equity.

The reason that blockchain seems to have a bright future in the banking sector is because of the benefits it can offer:

- Smarter and faster KYC
- Better due diligence
- Paper replaced by digitisation
- Lower overhead costs
- Lower fraud rates and security issues

However, as per the majority of banking leaders, it would take at least a decade for blockchain to show worldwide financial adoption.

- **Instant Payments**

The distributed ledger technology on which blockchain is based offers the facility of secure and smooth peer to peer transactions. This feature can have vast implications in the conventional payment systems, where a specific percentage of the transaction amount is allocated as a processing fee and transferred to the platform. By using blockchain, instant payments may be carried out on a global scale without any transaction or processing fee. However, the instant payment system hasn't seen mass adoption of blockchains due to the current low speed of transactions on the blockchain.

Therefore, similar to the blockchain, but free from their transaction speed issues, many platforms have emerged that promise faster transactions globally. Some of them are the lightning network, which uses smart contracts for instant transactions. Other is the Raiden network, which operates on the Ethereum blockchain and ensures scalable and near-instant transactions with a small value of transaction fees.

Government

- **Voting**

In spite of many security provisions the electronic voting machines and booths have been subjected to various security breaches, even in technologically advanced nations. To tackle such issues a blockchain backed project called Agora came up for enabling tamper-proof and transparent voting during the Presidential elections of Sierra Leone in 2018.
However, its use was denied by the government. Currently, the voting blockchain technology is still in its cradle stage and is a controversial subject in legislation, therefore suffers from the absence of mass adoption.

- **Border Control**

Immigration has risen as a hot topic in many advanced nations, mostly in Europe and the United States. As a result, all these nations have started feeling the need for dedicating more and more resources for maintaining border control. Since blockchain can be used for identification without involving any third party like the government, this technology is being tested for checking the citizenship of the immigrants safely and securely.

The enhanced privacy feature is further compounded by the use of smart contracts, which could be integrated with the biometric information. As the government would alter its immigration policies, the data in the smart contract algorithm could be effectively updated and help in storing and securing the identity data in an immutable, decentralised ledger.

One such project, which came up with the idea of using blockchain for border security, is Factom, which won the contract from the US Department of Homeland Security. The aim of this project is to securely collect and package the data of the immigrants and the citizens on the blockchain platform.

- **Education**

The ability of blockchain to store the data in a secure, cheap and immutable manner has made this technology particularly lucrative for the educational sector. The Holberton School of Software Engineering in San Francisco has gained prominence as the first school globally to issue certificates for its students on a blockchain platform.

The blockchain technology can find another educational use of providing lower tuition rates to the students. Currently, more and more families are demanding a less expensive and faster alternative to the educational system prevalent today. This is particularly true taking into consideration the exorbitant fees charged by the US educational institutions.
A project named ODEM is starting to counteract the follies present in the current educational system. This project would use smart contracts for exchanging educational courses between the students and the lecturers at much lower prices. At present, the network consists of more than 200 professors hailing from the leading universities in the US.

Retail and Manufacturing Sector

- **Supply Chain**

Supply chain, which generally spans various and far-reaching geographic regions, forms an extremely complex aspect of the manufacturing and retail industry. The most significant issues with the supply chain are the involvement of multiple parties, many invoices, a dearth of transparency and fake inventories. The situation is further worsened by the lengthy period in which all these operations and steps operate.

Through blockchain, which offers enhanced security, immutable data storage and transparency, it would be easy to track the merchandise along with its owner and the state from where it would be travelling.

At present, blockchain is being used in the food sector which demands better means of tracing the origins of the foods for protecting the health of consumers and maintaining trust in the merchandise. Hyperledger is such a project which is composed of multiple blockchains and other related open source tools. It claims that it would use this decentralised technology to tackle the illegal fishing issues plaguing the fishing industry.

- **Healthcare**

Healthcare is another industry that would benefit from the use of blockchain technology. This sector involves the use of multiple patient records, many of which need a high level of privacy, while being shared with multiple entities like doctors. Besides, the medical industry is on the verge of adopting the IoT infrastructure, which would enable the connection of multiple objects like a tablet, mobile and other medical devices to an accessible internet source. However, the network would also become more prone to security breaches by hackers if it adopts the IoT system. Another challenge of the medical sector is Medicare fraud which amounted to a total value of $16.2 billion in the US during the year 2016.

Therefore, blockchain would be a boon to this industry, as it would enable the secure storage of medical data while verifying it without involving a third party. At present MIT has begun a project named as MedRec which strives for the integration of the medical field with the blockchain technology.

The blockchain is much beyond bitcoin.

It is apparent that blockchain is just at the cusp of major resurgence with a wide range of industries adopting this technology for its plethora of benefits. At present, where the applications of blockchain have far exceeded that of conventional cryptocurrency uses, it wouldn't be wrong to quote Sally Davies, the famous technology reporter:

"Blockchain is to bitcoin what the internet is to email. A big electronic system on top of which you can build applications. Currency is just one."

Chapter 3 - Components of Blockchain

The Blockchain can be a bit overwhelming from the technology point of view. However, taking one component at a time makes it easier. At a high level, it makes the use of distributed computing fundamentals combined with cryptographic concepts (digital signatures, cryptographic hash functions, and asymmetric key cryptography). These two components are then combined with record keeping concepts like a public ledger. Let's first look at some building blocks of the technology.

Cryptographic Hash Functions
An essential component of the blockchain is the usage of cryptographic hash functions for several operations. Hashing is a process of applying a mathematical formula to a given input to produce an output string of a particular size, e.g. 256 bytes, known as digest or message digest for the input of any size – a file, image or text. No matter how long is the input, the output will always be of the same size and no two inputs, no matter how big or small, can have the same output ever.

Key features of the Cryptographic hash functions are:
- The cryptographic hash functions are resistant to pre-image. It means that these functions are one way; it is computationally impossible to figure out the input data for a give output data. For example, for a given a digest it is impossible to find x where Hash(x) = Digest.
- Easily Verifiable – if you have the input data, you can quickly find the output digest using the hash function and verify that output has been calculated from the given input.

- They are also resistant to a collision. It means no two different inputs can result in the same output. In simple words, it is impossible to get two inputs that give the same hash.

Cryptographic hash functions execute several tasks within a network of the blockchain. Some of the functions are as follows:
- The creation of a unique identifier of each entity in the network.
- Securing the Block data: A publishing node hashes the block data and stores it with the block header.
- Address derivation: Public addresses of the users are also derived using a cryptographic hash.

Asymmetric Key Cryptography

The blockchain technology uses asymmetric key cryptography to generate a pair of keys – a private key and a public key. Both of them mathematically relate to each other. The public key is open and the private key is kept secret. It is impossible to derive the private key based on the information of the public key even if there is a correlation between these two keys. A user can encrypt any data with the private key and data can only be decrypted by the public key.

Asymmetric key cryptography enables a trust relationship between the users. It offers a mechanism to examine the authenticity and integrity of deals and allows the transactions to stay open/public. The transactions have digital signatures. In simple words, one can encrypt a transaction with his private key and decrypt it with the general key as the public key is open and encrypting the transaction with a personal key ensures that the signer/user has access to the private key.

In brief, the use of asymmetric key cryptography in blockchain networks is as follows:

- Privates keys are used to sign the transaction and sent to the network. It not only protects the message but is also used as the identifier of the sender.
- Public keys are used to validate the message and again user identification.

Addresses

Many networks in the blockchain technology use an address which is a short, alphanumeric string of characters derived from the users' public key of the blockchain network. It is done with the use of a cryptographic hash function and some extra data like a version number. In comparison with the public keys, addresses are shorter. One method for the generation of an address is as follows:

- Create a public key
- Apply a cryptographic hash function to it
- Convert the hash into text

Public Key → Cryptographic hash function → Address

Every blockchain implementation has a different way to obtain an address. In public blockchain networks it is easy to create an account anonymously, and a user can generate several pairs of asymmetric keys. Therefore, addresses allow the verification of pseudo-anonymity to a level. Often, an address is transformed into a QR code for making the use more convenient. For a user the address may act as a public facing identifier in the blockchain network.

Within a blockchain network, the users are not a single source for addresses. In Ethereum smart contracts are accessible with a particular address, which is known as a contract account. With the deployment of a smart contract this contract account is generated.

The contract account permits the execution of the contract when it has a transaction and additional smart contracts.

Transactions

A transaction corresponds to a deal executed between two parties. In the case of cryptocurrencies, for instance, a transaction means transfers of the cryptocurrency between the users of a blockchain network. For a B2B scenario, a transaction is a way to record the activities happening on physical or digital assets.

In the blockchain, a user provides transaction details to the network. The details consist of the user's address, a digital signature, user's public key, and transaction outputs along with transaction inputs.

Inputs – The inputs are a catalogue of the digital assets that are transferred. A transaction will locate the digital asset source – either the prior transaction in the ledger or the newly generated asset. There is no change to the overall digital assets, only the transfer of the assets to one or more parties. In the case of cryptocurrency, it means that there is no addition to or deduction from the existing digital assets. As an alternative a particular digital asset can be divided into several new digital assets, or many digital assets can be placed together to form some new digital assets. The sender has to offer the proof of ownership to the referred inputs.

Outputs – The outputs are the accounts that are of the recipients of the digital assets along with the information on the assets being received. Every output states the number of the assets that are to be transferred to the new proprietor, a set of conditions regarding the value and the identifier of the original proprietors.

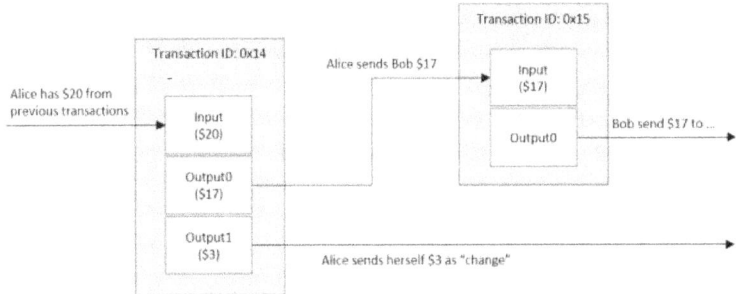

Transactions can be used to transfer data while primarily used to transmit digital assets. In general, one may merely wish to publicly and permanently post the data on the blockchain. In smart contracts transactions are used to transfer the data, process that data and record the results on this technology. For instance, a transaction is used to modify a feature of a digital asset like the shipment location within the supply chain system based on blockchain technology.

Ensuring the authenticity and validity of a transaction is essential. The network validates the legitimacy of trade by making sure the transaction is as per the protocol, smart contract or formalised data, needs particular to the implementation of the blockchain. It also ensures that the sender of the digital assets has a right of ownership to those assets. The validation is done using the digital signatures of the sender.

Ledgers

A *ledger* is usually a set of transactions. Before the advent of the computer or blockchain technology, people use pen and paper ledgers to keep a record of trades or the exchange of goods & services. In today's world, professionals use an extensive database operated and owned by a centralised, reliable third party to store the ledgers. The third party does it on behalf of the users of a community.

The interest to explore the distributed ledger ownership has always been there, and the blockchain technology strengthens such an approach by using both a distributed ownership and a distributed physical architecture. The distributed physical architecture consists of a large collection of computers in comparison with centralised ownership. Security, transparency, possible trust and reliability concerns are big drivers in advancing distributed ledger technology.

Here is a comparison between a manual centralised ledger and a blockchain ledger:

Manual/Central Ledger	Blockchain Ledger
There is a high chance of the centrally owned manual ledger being lost or destroyed.	Less or no chance of data loss. It allows every user to update his/her copy of the ledger.
It is a homogeneous network. The network, software and hardware infrastructure are the same.	It is a heterogeneous network. The software, hardware and network infrastructure are different.
It has specific geographic locations, i.e. a country.	It comprises of different geographic nodes across the world. It works on peer-peer-fashion.
The transaction is not transparent. The users must believe that the owner is updating the transaction.	In the blockchain network, every transaction is transparent. The users have information for every transaction.

Manual/Central Ledger	Blockchain Ledger
In the manual ledger the transaction may not be complete. The user has to believe that each transaction is included.	It has a list of all the accepted transactions and it informs the users when a new node/transaction is added.
The transaction data may be altered and the users have to keep faith in the owner that he/she is not altering transaction data.	It works on cryptographic mechanisms like digital signatures and cryptographic hash functions to make the ledger tamper resistant.

Blocks

In blockchain, generally the transactions are not committed to the ledger individually, they are collected together for a certain time interval which differs in each implementation, and then committed together as a block.

Each block in the blockchain has the same components as mentioned in the figure:

- A block number
- The hash function of the prior block
- Nonce, known as a random number
- Transaction data
- Timestamp with the detail of block creation time
- The hash of the present block

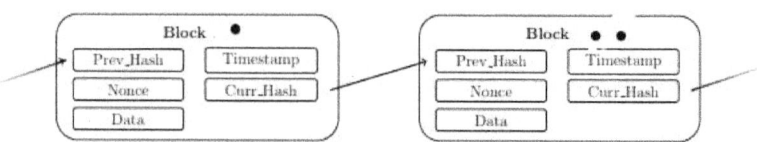

In simple language, each block has a block number which is connected with the prior hash as well as the present hash. It helps in determining the order in which the transaction occurred. The timestamp helps in determining the time at which block was committed. The data consists of the transactions which could include almost everything. Last but not least, there is *nonce*, which is a random number generated when creating each block. The nonce plays a critical role in some of the blockchains as whosoever finds the correct nonce gets to commit the block and gets a reward.

There is one exception – the first block also called genesis block. It is the only one which slightly differs from all other blocks, and it has no prior block, and hence no block hash.

Chaining blocks

Blocks are placed together via every block consisting the hash digest of the previous block's header, hence forming the chain and the name blockchain. A block will have a different hash if a change is made in the prior published block. As a result it would cause all succeeding blocks to be invalidated. Therefore, it becomes extremely difficult to fraudulently change data in any of the previous blocks making the ledger tamper-proof. Even if one of the nodes does change the data on its copy, the other nodes will reject it as it will not match their copy of the ledger.

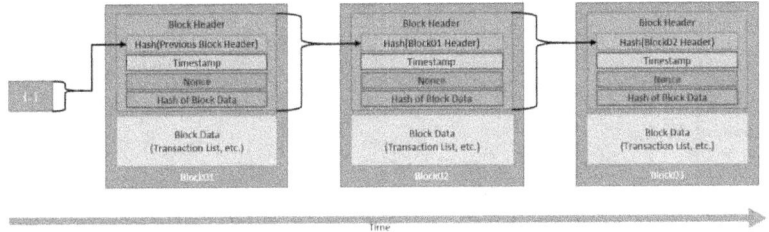

Smart Contracts

Smart contracts support exchange money, shares, property or anything important in a conflict-free and transparent way without any intervention of a middleman. In technical terms, these are pieces of code that reside on the blockchain and execute pre-defined transactions when a certain condition is met on the network.

For instance, one individual takes an apartment on rent from the owner. The individual participates in blockchain and uses a cryptocurrency for the payment. The owner provides a digital entry key which the smart contract delivers to an individual on the rental start date. The smart contract sends a refund to the individual if the digital key does not come on time. The technology holds the release of both the key and the fee until the respective date if the owner sends the key before the date fixed for renting. Based on the If-Then premise, the system ensures a faultless delivery. The owner is sure to get paid if he/she gives the key to the renter/individual.

How does it all work together?

Now let's put all these technologies together and see how they work.

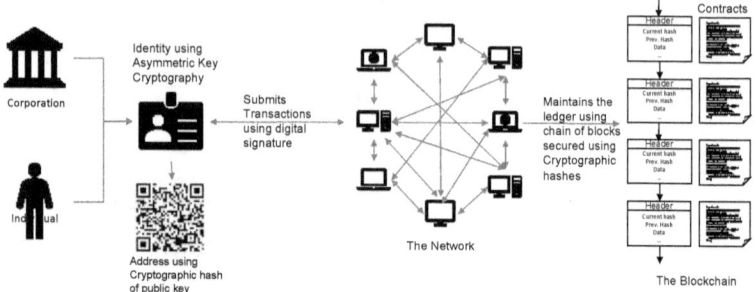

The Network

The Blockchain

Note: There is only one ledger/chain shown in the image for simplicity. In reality, every node shown in the network has the same copy of the ledger or chain and is maintained locally by each node.

Consensus Mechanism

Now that you have understood all the components of the blockchain, the question is that who gets to commit the block of transactions to the chain. It cannot be a single entity that commits the block all the time because that will defeat the very purpose of the technology. This is where consensus algorithms come into play. The blockchain consensus is the process of the agreement by all/set of parties on the validity of a block (set of transactions) and the inclusion of that block on the chain.

There could be thousands of nodes in the network, and everyone cannot be allowed to propose valid transaction-set at the same time. Hence there is a need to select a node for proposing the new block randomly. The random selection of proposer node ensures that there is no centralised control. Random selection of the node is made in many ways, and that's what are the different algorithms in the blockchain consensus.

The very first proposed algorithm is **Proof of Work (PoW).** This algorithm requires nodes to solve a cryptographic puzzle, and whichever node solves it first gets the right to propose the next block. The randomness in this algorithm is created by the fact that the cryptographic puzzle can only be solved by brute force, so it is almost impossible for the same node to be selected to propose two blocks in a row. Once a randomly picked node proposes the block, the rest of the nodes validates the puzzle solution and accepts the new block.

This algorithm has maximum randomness and hence the reliability. However, there is a lot of power wastage as all nodes are racing to solve the puzzle.

Hence the second algorithm getting popular is **Proof-of-Stake (PoS).** In this mechanism, the nodes that want to be a block proposer has to block some cryptocurrency which will ensure that reliability and honesty of the node. Here the randomness is provided by the fact that there could be many nodes willing to stake money. The highest bidder gets to propose the next block. The randomness reduces to only a certain set of nodes having a lot of cryptocurrencies, but still provide the reliability, because if these nodes behave maliciously the value of cryptocurrency will go down. And they can be penalised as well.

A variation of Proof-of-Stake is **Delegated-Proof-of-Stake (DPoS).** In this case the nodes putting the stake does not propose the block themselves, but they further nominate the nodes who proposes the next block. The randomness is fairly similar to what we have in PoS algorithm.

Proof-of-Authority (PoA) is another algorithm where the proposer nodes are pre-defined. This algorithm has the least randomness as nodes are pre-authorised and known. This brings in a lot of centralisation characteristics into the blockchain which is not always desirable. However, there are use cases for such consensus as well.

Intel implemented another way to get randomness is blockchain consensus, based on the wait time on the CPU of the node. This algorithm is known as **Proof-of-Elapsed-Time (PoET).** This, however, is only available on Intel machines.

Another popular algorithm is **Practical Byzantine Fault Tolerance (pBFT).** This algorithm does not use a single proposer node of a block; rather every node validates the transaction at the same time and majority vote required for the block to be included on the chain.

Although there are many algorithms in various stages of development/proposal, the only proven algorithm is Proof of Work and is used in the majority of cryptocurrencies.

Chapter 4 - Popular Implementations

Popular Blockchain implementations and their comparison

Blockchain technology is providing a new tool to solve problems in a way people could not do before. When the blockchain comes into mind, most of the people think of bitcoin, which is the most popular implementation of this technology. However, there are several other implementations available. Some of them are presently running while some are still in the development process. These different implementations differ from each other regarding their purpose, operation, ease of participation, and so on. It is essential to be familiar with dissimilarities between these implementations before determining the right implementation for an application.

The purpose of any blockchain framework is the essential point to consider for selection, but many developers overlook it. Most of the existing blockchains are for cryptocurrencies, and many of them use the bitcoin codebase. These blockchains can be used for non-monetary applications by saving the application data within transactions.

The next point to consider for the blockchain implementation is the ease of participation. For instance, running a full node may be a requirement for connecting to a blockchain network. The node saves blocks and the whole history of transactions. Some of the blockchains that have clients from small business industries allow the entry to the network without downloading the entire transaction history. Besides, it is crucial to know the ecosystem of the blockchain is open to everyone or closed for a group. For the creation of a similar but not identical blockchain implementation, developers can fork the open source code.

The governance is the point which needs consideration for a blockchain implementation. It influences operations and functions. Therefore, one must think of who governs access to the ecosystem and has a crucial role in making decisions for the changes in the network. Most of the blockchains need consensus from all the users/participants to agree to a change in the blockchain. With less control in the blockchain network, someone may have difficulty in utilising the blockchain for their application.

The performance is also crucial for blockchain implementation. The measurement of the rate of transaction acceptance in the network is essential. The measure includes transaction speed, the data amount required for saving, the amount of bandwidth and the way of saving data. It can also consist of the speed in the addition of new blocks, transaction rates, and transaction size.

Based on these criteria, here are some popular blockchain implementations that are going to be explained:

1. Bitcoin
2. Ethereum
3. Hyperledger
4. R3-Corda
5. TradeLens
6. Quorum
7. Ripple
8. Others

Bitcoin
It is a digital currency and payments system which allows users to make transactions without the involvement of a third party or system. Its source code is the first implementation of the blockchain. The bitcoin blockchain saves transaction data, which denotes the currency amount transferred between two or more accounts. However, there is a way to encode additional data into

transactions, i.e. OP_RETURN. One can use the OP_RETURN to store arbitrary data of up to 40 bytes. Still, the primary goal of bitcoin is to the transaction of digital currency.

Bitcoin's currency is the *bitcoin* (BTC, ฿ or Ⓑ). Its smallest unit is *Satoshi,* named after Satoshi Nakamoto, the author of the white paper, *Bitcoin – A Peer to Peer Electronic Cash System.* It is equivalent to 1/100,000,000th of a bitcoin.

Based on open source software, the bitcoin protocol is the most familiar way for the users to participate in the blockchain. The participation takes place with the exchange of bitcoins. To obtain bitcoin, a participant generates private and public keys. With the public key, the user produces a bitcoin address, and others use it to send this cryptocurrency. Several third party sources are available for obtaining bitcoin at the present exchange rate.

Running a node is another way to interact with bitcoin. The node saves the complete bitcoin blockchain along with all transaction history.

The main blockchain and the testnet blockchain are two different networks in bitcoin. Both use the same protocol, but the first one (main blockchain) is valid for payment in the real world. The primary purpose of the testnet is to permit users to learn how to use bitcoin applications without doing any harm to the main blockchain.

There is a lot more to explain about bitcoin. However, here is its summary:

Bitcoin	
Purpose	Cryptocurrency
Type of data to be	Cryptocurrency transactions, additional

saved/store	data in coinbase or OP_RETURN transactions
Scripting language	Script
Open Ecosystem	Yes
Participation process	Download the source code and run a node. Get currency from online trading service.
Native currency	bitcoin
Registration authority	N/A
Transparency in making decisions	Yes
Block release time	10 minutes
Transaction Size	200 bytes minimum, 250 bytes avg
Transaction Rate	3 tx/sec. Avg. 7 tx/sec.Theoretical maximum
Consensus Model	Nodes verify blocks and transactions and select blockchain with the most blocks.
Mining	Proof of work

Ethereum

In 2014, the founders of Ethereum (Gavin Wood, Vitalik Buterin and Jeffrey Wilcke) started developing a next generation blockchain. The principal reason behind the development of Ethereum was to implement a Turing-complete smart contracts language, which was one of the most significant drawbacks of the bitcoin protocol.

As an open blockchain platform, Ethereum permits anyone to create and use a decentralised application based on blockchain technology. Like the bitcoin, no one can own or control Ethereum. Unlike the bitcoin protocol, it is flexible and adaptable. Instead of going to elaborate details, here is the summary of Ethereum:

Ethereum	
Purpose	Run smart contracts
Type of data to be saved/store	Cryptocurrency, digital assets, smart contracts
Scripting language	Solidity, Serpent, LLL
Open ecosystem	Yes
Participation process	Download the source code and run a node. Get currency from online trading service.
Native currency	ether (ETH, ETC)
Registration authority	N/A
Transparency in making decisions	Yes
Block release time	12 seconds
Transaction Size	Theoretically no max (actual max: 89 kB)

Transaction Rate	Theoretically no maximum
Consensus Model	Similar to bitcoin but uses Ethereum Virtual Machine
Mining	Proof of work using Ethash algorithm

Hyperledger

Hyperledger is an open source and joint collaborative effort developed to go forward in the cross-industry blockchain technologies. It is a worldwide collaboration including the industry leaders from the fields like banking, supply chains, IoT, finance and manufacturing. Under it the Hyperledger has several projects as per the submission of the member companies. Intel has submitted Sawtooth Lake which is one of the major projects under this coalition. Hyperledger Fabric is the most commonly used framework.

Key points of Hyperledger Fabric

Hyperledger Fabric	
Purpose	Enable the creation of blockchains for industry use cases
Type of data to be saved/store	Chaincode (i.e. smart contracts)
Scripting language	Go (golang), Java (in progress)
Open ecosystem	Yes
Participation process	- Create a new blockchain: Download source and follow instructions. - Join existing network: Register with a

	proof of identity to the network membership services
Native currency	N/A
Registration authority	Yes, Pluggable
Transparency in making decisions	Yes
Block release time	Unknown
Transaction Size	Unknown
Transaction Rate	> 10k tx/sec.
Consensus Model	Pluggable consensus framework; Two inbuilt mechanisms provided: Dummy and PBFT plugin

R3-Corda

R3-Corda is a distributed ledger technology built for the financial services industry. This platform is maintained by a consortium of more than 200 financial services organisations and is led by an organisation named R3.

Key points of R3-Corda

R3-Corda	
Purpose	Distributed Ledger for Financial Services
Type of data to be saved/store	Digital Assets and Smart Contracts

Scripting language	Kotlin, targeting JVM and JavaScript
Open ecosystem	Yes
Participation process	- Create a blockchain: Download source and follow instructions. - Join existing network: Register with a proof of identity to the network membership services
Native currency	N/A
Registration authority	Unknown
Transparency in making decisions	Unknown
Block release time	Unknown
Transaction Size	Unknown
Transaction Rate	N/A
Consensus Model	Transaction Validity, Transaction Uniqueness

TradeLens

TradeLens is an open industry solution for supply chain (mainly shipping). This platform promotes a more predictable, efficient and safe exchange of information for encouraging greater collaboration and reliability in the supply chain across the world.

It shares real time and end-to-end supply chain information among transportation providers, cargo owners, 3PLs and more. With it the transfer of trade documents from organisations to trade finance automate custom clearance and is seamless and secured. With this blockchain implementation there is a significant improvement in the physical as well as the financial asset with more complete operational data. Managing the entire operation within the stated time becomes more effortless.

Key Points of TradeLens
- TradeLens is a joint venture of IBM and Maersk.
- It enables digital collaboration across several parties engaged in global trade.
- It allows tracking critical data for each shipment in a supply chain. It offers an absolute record among all the involved parties.
- During a trial period of 12 months, IBM and Maersk worked with many ecosystem partners to find out solutions on how to prevent delays due to errors in documents, information delays and other obstructions.
- This blockchain platform aims to capture more than 154 million events in shipping. The growth rate is 1 million a day.
- It can help in managing the arrival time of vessels, documents (commercial invoice, custom release and lading bills), container gate-ins.

Quorum

Quorum, developed by J.P. Morgan, is an Ethereum based blockchain platform. It is one of the significant steps taken for the adoption of blockchain technology in the financial sector. It is permission based and is an enterprise focused blockchain infrastructure mainly designed and developed for commercial use cases.

Primary features of Quorum
- Higher performance
- Multiple voting based consensus mechanisms
- Network/Peer permissions management

- Transaction and contract privacy

Key points of Quorum:

Quorum	
Purpose	Provide a secured and safe blockchain infrastructure
Type of data to be saved/store	Smart Contracts, transaction data
Scripting language	C++, Python
Open ecosystem	Yes
Participation process	Get the source, follow the instructions for registration and start transferring money
Native currency	N/A
Registration authority	Unknown
Transparency in making decisions	Unknown
Block release time	N/A
Transaction Size	Unknown
Transaction Rate	2.3 thousand per second

Ripple

Released in 2012, it is an RTGS (real time gross settlement system), remittance and currency exchange network. It is a ledger governed by a network of independent validation servers. The validating server can be anyone, from professionals to banks.

This blockchain platform enables inexpensive and fast transactions between two parties. It allows the exchange of any currency from gold to fiat, or to even airline miles. This open source protocol/platform relieves people from the waiting time and traditional transfer fee.

Key points of Ripple

Ripple	
Purpose	Move money across the world as fast as possible
Type of data to be saved/stored	Smart Contracts, Transaction Data
Scripting language	C++
Open ecosystem	Yes
Participation process	Get the source, follow the instructions for registration and start transferring money
Native currency	XRP
Registration authority	Unknown
Transparency in making decisions	Unknown

Block release time	N/A
Transaction Size	Unknown
Transaction Rate	50000 transactions per second

Others

Apart from the above, there are more blockchain implementations. Some of them are as follows:

Altcoin - It is an alternative to bitcoin and consists of cryptocurrencies like litecoin and dogecoin.

HydraChain - As a joint venture of Ethereum and Brainbot Technologies, HydraChain is an extension of Ethereum blockchain platform.

OpenChain - Developed by Coinprism, OpenChain aims to support businesses in issuing and managing their digital assets.

SideChain - As a blockchain platform, it allows its users to validate data from other blockchains and assets can be imported from and returned to other chains.

Steem - As a blockchain based social media platform, it allows users to get rewards for posting meaningful content.

Lisk - It allows users to create their applications separately on SideChain that relate to mainchain or main blockchain.

IOTA - It is a new kid in the blockchain implementation. It is based on a blockless distributed ledger, which is known as *Tangle*.

Chapter 5 - Blockchain and Enterprise IT

What can Blockchain do across the Enterprise?

Blockchain through its multiple functionalities like cryptography, hashing, consensus algorithms and smart contracts can change the way of business operations several organisations have been doing traditionally. An enterprise can enhance its reliability, security, automation of business transaction data, and audibility by integrating their core systems with blockchain. Besides, it can reduce the dependency on the third parties. This technology can connect to most of the business applications such as enterprise resource planning (ERP), customer relationship manager (CRM), SCM, MIS, EAI, CMS, and e-commerce. Its integration will enable the mainstream client to attain business success.

Blockchain and SCM

SCM or *Supply Chain Management* offers an entire control over the production, transportation and distribution of products. With this IT solution, enterprises cut additional costs and supply products to clients faster. With the support of this software solution, businesses have strict control over internal production, inside inventories, outer inventories (of vendors), distribution and sales. Supply Chain Management helps in increasing revenues, reducing costs and impacting a firm's bottom line.

Each time a product is with a different owner there is a need for documentation for creating the whole history of a product, from manufacturing to supply. Integrating a blockchain system will bring a dramatic change in reducing delivery delays, extra costs and human error. Experts suggest that blockchain would be a widespread *Supply Chain Operating System*. Blockchain technology can enhance the following tasks of a firm dealing with supply chain:

- Recording the transfer and quantity of assets such as trailers, pallets and containers have become more comfortable. They shift between the nodes of the supply chain.
- Tracking orders of purchase, receipts and change and shipment notifications along with other trade documents become faster.
- Handing over and verifying certifications or some specific attributes of a physical product. For instance, determining whether a food product is a fair trade or organic, it is efficient and less time-consuming.
- Connecting consignments to barcodes, serial numbers and digital tags such as RFID is more hassle free.
- Sharing information manufacturing, assembly, maintenance and delivery process of products with vendors and suppliers are safe and secured.

Blockchain enhances the value of ERP

ERP or *Enterprise Resource Planning* offers countless benefits to an organisation/firm. By centralising all business data, it allows firms to have complete control over the internal operations and enables informed decisions for the future. It permits to update all data in real time which is critical for smooth business operations in all sectors. Besides, it supports having constant communication between different departments in a firm, and this eliminates the risk of errors.

The integration of blockchain takes these benefits of ERP solution to the next level. With it enterprises get an ability to selectively expose the data across several organisations without exposing the ERP to the outside world. Although middleware can also achieve the data exposure however, it being a centralized source will still not have the trust that blockchain can provide. By integrating a blockchain technology, the optimisation of business operations in many firms becomes smoother. A company has no risk while sharing data.

Blockchain and CRM

CRM is for saving and retrieving the records of held interactions and transactions between clients and suppliers. CRM and other peripheral technologies, the front-office system along with the back one, has become more intertwined. As a result, many big companies struggle to get a 360-degree view of the customer.

Integrating a blockchain technology with CRM ensures having more data consistency without making any change in the CRM. Blockchain provides a flexible foundation for data management. Due to its distributed and open design capability, blockchain is easy to implement with CRM solution. Integrating blockchain with Customer Relationship Management makes interacting with customers more comfortable. Getting information about existing as well as probable customers will be convenient. Apart from acceleration in data aggression, CRM with blockchain will enhance insights and support firms to provide highly accurate and personalised offers to their customers.

Blockchain and E-commerce

E-commerce selling has existed for more than three decades, and the evolution in this sector has been excellent. Technological advancements have influenced this sector over the years and blockchain is one of those technologies which is going to revolutionise e-commerce with its unique potential. It has a lot to offer to support e-commerce firms transform their short as well as long-term challenges.

Before stating what blockchain can do for this sector, have a look at the challenges most e-commerce companies are facing.

- The sector has been highly competitive and the competition is getting stricter day by day as players of different scales offer the same products and services. Therefore, companies have to adopt smarter technologies and business models to stay in the market.
- Another big challenge is the involvement of middlemen who take a massive amount of earnings as a sale comes to a close. For example, sellers have to give a transaction processing fee to ease payments for transaction completion.
- The safety of consumer data is also a big concern for e-commerce companies as they have to earn the trust of their customers. They have to ensure that their details are entirely safe. For this the e-commerce businesses invests a considerable amount of money in data encryption along with allied measures to prohibit hacking.
- Online selling is a complex process as it includes an extensive range of operations like payments, supply chain and logistics. Managing all these operations and the involvement of mediators is a critical challenge for the sector.

Since these challenges have been faced by the sellers from the very beginning, so they have been in search of a solution/technology that can enable them to handle the same.

How Blockchain fits in e-commerce

The blockchain is a natural fit for the e-commerce industry as it is well-designed for saving transaction data. The data is not necessarily financial but can be a separate action which needs an absolute record consisting of operations related to order fulfilment and payment.

- Integrating blockchain with e-commerce offers alternative payment methods. Customers can choose bitcoin for payment as they do by opting for Stripe, PayPal or other payment processors.

- With a blockchain technology a transaction will be faster and the process involved in it will be simplified. It will be beneficial for merchants and buyers as well. At present millions of transactions are taking place in a second.
- The integration of a blockchain technology ensures the complete payment security. Cryptocurrencies do not expose personal information as well as sensitive data such as card number.
- The implementation of a blockchain technology into an e-commerce application ensures having an enhanced order fulfilment strategy. As each block in a blockchain the network connects to the previous one, so an e-commerce company has a visible chain of transactions enabling it to boost the fulfilment process of order.

Conclusion

Apart from cryptocurrency, the research and development work is going on in blockchain. Some IT enterprise solutions have incorporated this technology, and some are looking at possibilities of what can be done.

Chapter 6 - Blockchain in Financial Services

Blockchain in Banking and Insurance

Blockchain has been acknowledged for bringing transparency in almost all business transactions. As an open source technology, it is going to revolutionise the economy across the globe. With its cryptographic techniques, this technology assists in tracking all types of interactions and transactions. Besides, it simplifies the process of collaboration.

Blockchain in Banking

The technology provides the public ledger, a log consisting of metadata how and when a transaction takes place. Moreover, the ledger is open to all. Being cryptographically safe, technology prevents altering present and past transactions. Besides, it keeps a copy of every one of a distributed network's data within it.

Due to transparency, reduced operating cost and related features of blockchain, banks are keen to implement it. Implementing a blockchain technology will help banks increase profit and value.

Challenges of the banking sector

With the advancement in technology, the banking sector has changed its operational process. However, this industry has been facing challenges after a dream run in 2000. At present, banks have many problems, and some of the major ones are as follows:

- *Not enough profit* – In fact, banks and financial firms are making no profit in spite of banking profitability headlines. They are not getting the right return on their investment or equity.
- *Customer expectations* – Today's world is all about the consumer experience. Several banks feel pressure as they

are not offering the banking services as per their customers' expectations, mainly in a technological aspect.

- *Throat-cut competition* – Banks are facing fierce competition from FinTech (financial technology) companies that use software-based financial services. The rise in the popularity of FinTech companies is threatening the way traditional banking has been operating. This is a big confrontation for conventional banks. Besides, the financial sector is getting divided into small areas like home loans, payment banks, and small financial companies offering banking services.
- *Regulatory pressure* – Regulatory needs are on the rise and banks have to invest a large part of their budget on being compliant and on developing processes and systems to stay updated with the escalating needs.
- *Microeconomic risk* – Uncertainties in the microeconomic atmosphere along with constant and high debt levels across corporate, farmers and consumer sectors affect banks a lot. Due to these, there is significant instability in this industry. Increase in NPAs and debts slows down the growth rate and harms the economy worldwide.
- *Political interference* – Bankers in many countries, including China and India, have expressed concern that governments interfere in banking operations for several reasons. Some primary purposes are to rise in investor protection, increase revenue at the time of the budget and build a tax base at the national level. The uncertainty in many political atmospheres including the Middle East, Europe, and South Asia and upcoming elections disrupt banking operations and lend policies and taxation.
- *Criminality* – Cyberattacks are the main concern for the banking sector in today's world. Banks have many responses that state they are not well equipped to prohibit attacks from organised criminals, opportunistic hackers or government supported corporate spying. Banks with

updated technological solutions are strong. However, they need to be more powerful and stronger to stand against criminality.

How can Blockchain help banks to face their ongoing challenges?

Blockchain technology can probably transform the banking industry. Here are some substantial ways that it can change the financial sector:

Fraud reduction

Even though being a new technology, and in the development stage, its ability to bring fraud down in the banking industry is getting much attention. It is because around 45% of financial middlemen like money transfer services and stock exchanges suffer a lot from economic crime each year. Most of the banks across the globe are based on a centralised database which is more susceptible to cyberattacks. The centralised database consists of one failure point instead of several ones. As a hacker breaches one system, he/she gets access to the entire system. With the implementation of blockchain technology, the banking system would have several points, and hence, it will be quite hard for hackers to get access.

KYC (Know your customer)

According to a Thomson Reuters survey, banks spend from 60 to 500 million US dollars to keep their KYC data and allied regulations updated. These regulations are meant for reducing terrorism activities and money laundering cases. Besides, these help the banks in identifying and verifying their clients. With the implementation of blockchain, there would be an independent examination of a client by a bank, and other banks could use the same data and escape themselves from doing the same from the beginning. It would help to reduce administrative expenses for compliance departments of the banking sector.

Smart contracts

Blockchain can save any digital information such as computer code, so it makes users have smart contracts. The computer code would be programmed to build settlements or do monetary transactions once a fixed set of criteria is attained.

Payments

With the integration of blockchain, the banking sector will have a transformed payment process. The banks will have lower costs and higher security in processing payments between firms and their customers and even between banks. In the current banking network, there are many intermediaries for payment processing.

Trading platforms

It's thrilling to study the changes that might take place with the trading platforms if they are based on blockchain technology. Undoubtedly, integrating blockchain will dramatically reduce fraud and the threat of operational errors. The Australian Securities Exchange and NASDAQ are developing blockchain solutions to enhance efficiencies and reduce costs.

Banks using Blockchain technology

Many leading banks across the world have implemented blockchain technologies, and several are willing to turn to the same. Here are some banks that are currently using blockchain technology:

China Construction Bank

In September 2017, it implemented a blockchain technology by having a partnership with IBM. It was meant to improve service delivery and streamline the transaction process. With the support of a distributed ledger, the solution helps banks enhance service quality and customer experience. Besides, it helps in making processing time faster and transactions transparent.

HSBC Holdings

It is the only bank that performed the first trade monetary transaction in the world with the use of blockchain technology. According to HSBC Holdings, it is an increase in efficiency, especially international trade.

BNP Paribas
It is exploring this emerging technology to optimise internal and global treasury operations. Besides, it views the use of blockchain based solutions as a ground-breaking approach to counter business requirements and enhance operational efficiency. It is, as it offers a more integrated cash management process between businesses, permitting greater flexibility along with 24/7 service competencies.

Bank of America
It is also utilising a blockchain based solution to develop a secured, efficient and trustworthy way to save records and allow authorised parties to access.

2gether Bank
As the first Spanish blockchain bank, it permits customers to avail complete banking services with the single one interface. It aims to allow a client to manage, hire, and exchange financial as well as non-financial assets. The assets like gasoline, electricity and knowledge are tokenised and made available for the customers. The users have all these in their account at their fingertips.

Bankera
It is creating a digital bank to last for the whole era of blockchain.

*Polybius*It is an entirely digital bank. Users can access it anywhere through mobile. The users have permission to control, optimise and manage their finances, and they attain this by joining all the features of the contemporary banking system like Big Data, IoT, and blockchain based solutions.

Blockchain in Insurance

Like other business sectors, insurance has a close watch on what is going in blockchain and what this technology can do. For insurance businesses, this technology has many essential aspects. With its integration, the insurance sector will have benefits like risk hedging, automatic payrolls and asset tracking. Many big insurance companies have already adopted blockchain, and several are willing to do the same.

With its features, a blockchain technology seems to suit well within the existing models of insurance firms. It will permit them to produce customised insurance to the insurer, in spite of offering general insurances to each one. Besides, it will allow the mechanisation of several aspects of this industry. There will be a considerable reduction in paper consumption to depict all the concerned terms and conditions of the contract.

Industry Use Cases

The blockchain is considered as a transformative mechanism in insurance sectors like:

Crop Insurance

With the use of blockchain, insurance companies will be capable of automatically processing fraud crop insurance claims by working with weather experts.

Health Insurance

A blockchain network, which combines physicians, hospitals, lab vendors and insurers, would enable a smooth flow of health information for enhanced validation of claims.

Property and Casualty

With blockchain integration, insurance companies would be capable of processing claims within 48 hours.

Travel Insurance
The use of blockchain would help in developing an ecosystem with insurance agencies and travel departments to automate the claim process.

Blockchain transforming the present death registration and claim process
The process involved in a death claim has not been revolutionised much in recent decades in spite of technical incorporation and automation. For most of the insurance players, this remains an exhaustive, subject to fraud, and insufficient process. As a result, the claim process is being buried in paperwork. Before going ahead, here is what death claim process was, what it is, and what it will be.

Claims Processing: Yesterday & Tomorrow

The 70s	The 90s	Future
Paper based processing	Automated Processing	Beneficiary focused processing
Manual entry and data verification	Claim adjudication on rules based engines	The beneficiary would be at the centre of all processing
No smooth process flow. Case file documents reach at different times	Decrease in manual data entry	Beneficiary would have an improved experience
Information in disparate systems	Electronic documentation systems.	Enhanced on time disbursement

Complex maintenance of documents	Reduction in workforce for claims processing	Minimise touchpoints
Considerable manual effort for claim disbursement		Better fraud detection

The death registration process in the current world

With some deviations, the process of death registration around the world has almost the same flow. At a higher level, the process outline is as follows:

- The last attending physician certifies a statement with nature or cause of death.
- The statement is sent to the government authority, or government authorised funeral home to release the death certificate.

The procedure mentioned above may differ from one country to another as listed below:

- USA – A certified funeral director starts the process for the issuance of the death certificate and burial permit after receiving a request for the same. Also, the director sends both a burial permit and death certificate to the respective state health department.
- UK – For death certificate and burial permit, a person belonging to the dead submits a request to the local registry office with an attachment of a medical document signed by the last attending doctor. The office reviews the case and issues a death certificate.
- Japan – The last attending doctor prepares and signs the death certificate. A request form with documents for

identity and burial/cremation request is submitted at the municipal registration office.

The present death claim process
After receiving it the beneficiary submits the death certificate to the respective insurance company with a request to start processing the claim. The firm examines the details. This process from the beginning to claim payout takes a minimum of 15/20 days to a maximum of six months. Most of the insurers follow the same process across the world.

Current challenges of the insurance sector
Requesting a death certificate and filing a claim for the same is a tedious and lengthy process for the beneficiary at the time when he/she loses his/her loved one. Due to manual processing, getting the claim payout could take up to six months. Besides, the possibility of fraud is higher as several data sources are present in the current process. For Canadian and US insurers, around 10% claim costs are credited to fraudulent claims.

Points to consider for future-ready blockchain solutions
Based on several manual touchpoints in the death registration as well as death claim processes, the insurance sector needs an amalgamated, single procedure. It must ensure transparency and information accessible to multiple stakeholders. Developing such a solution may require consideration of the following points:

Protection and security of data
- Rule based processing should ensure regulatory compliance, data protection and restriction to access.
- Transaction data must be under the set regulations, and the solution can perform a compliance review.

Implementation of multiparty shared network

- It should allow multiple parties to have access to modify/write/view the transaction data. For instance, a hospital or physician should be able to share information on the death cause/nature with the funeral home, the state health department and the insurer.
- It should ensure data access to every concerned party at any time.

Disintermediation
- A common platform for all stakeholders. The stakeholders can modify the transaction data themselves.
- Trust building among all concerned parties.

A single process
- Establishment of a unique, streamlined process to combine both death registration and death claim procedures.

Use case in claim processing
A likely approach would be to develop a customised blockchain solution that can integrate both death registrations and death claim processes. The nodes on the developed blockchain solution for the insurance sector would be insurance companies, the beneficiary, funeral homes, hospitals/clinics and the state health department.

To comprehend the whole scenario, consider a death occurs in the USA. The steps in the planned re-engineered procedure consist of:

- Death takes place in a hospital. The hospital staff enters all the details (along with a cause/nature of death) of the dead into the hospital records. The IT system of that hospital would be incorporated with a blockchain network. The information would be shared onto the network once the details are entered into the hospital record. With the use of cryptographic hashing techniques, the system would ensure data security.

- The insurer would match the data with its company records. The planned solution would ensure that only intended persons/stakeholders would receive or access the transaction data. The insurer would contact the beneficiary to confirm the match, making it successful.
- The beneficiary would choose a funeral home and fill the form to start the death registration process. The planned blockchain solution would ensure that the data would be available to the funeral home and the insurer in a secured and safe way.
- The funeral home would receive the request from the beneficiary. The respective director would log onto a portal incorporated with a blockchain network. Based on the available details, the director would fill the death registration form without getting in touch with the hospital. It reduces the turnaround time.
- The director would share the death registration form with the health department for the generation of the death certificate. The documents from both the beneficiary and the funeral home are shared on the network.
- The insurer would match all the specific details after receiving the death claim and disburse the claim amount. With smart contracts, the insurer calculates the claim amount.
- On the receipt of the claim amount, the beneficiary would admit the receipt and conclude the process.

Like health insurance, other insurance fields like travel and crop have almost the same issues. The issues can be resolved with the integration of a respective blockchain technology/platform.

Insurers (insurance companies) using Blockchain technology

Many big insurers have started using a blockchain technology, and several others are planning to implant. Here are some major insurance players that are using a blockchain based solution:

AXA

This giant French insurer has launched an insurance product for flight delay insurance. This insurance product uses the Ethereum blockchain platform to save data and process payouts. Flyers use this insurance product as a smart insurance tool to ensure their tours if their flight is deferred. It keeps a record for the held insurance contract and works as a mechanism to trigger the payment to the flyers when their flights are late for more than two hours.

Dynamis

It wants to be the first peer to peer insurance firm. It will use the advantages of smart contracts. Through LinkedIn, users can identify or log in. For instance, claimants can examine the accuracy of the reimbursement received via a reputed LinkedIn based system.

Teambrella

Based on bitcoin, it is an insurance solution which permits users to form teams to offer coverage to one another. The rest team members chip in to provide it if a user needs compensation.

Algang

It is a DAO (decentralised autonomous organisation). It is an insurance pool discovery. A user can predict market trends and earn rewards for his/her prediction. With the utilisation of smart contracts, it can ensure any Internet of Things (IoT) device.

Allianz

It has been exploring the use of blockchain in the banking sector since 2015. Its blockchain prototype aims to offer a most systematic approach for self-insurance or captive policies. As per Allianz, it will support financial companies along with their subsidiaries without buying additional conventional policies.

Overall, a blockchain technology will support the banking and insurance sectors to reduce costs, prevent fraud, enhance customer trust and help them to be globalised and stay connected to the world. With advancement, which is going on, it will entirely transform these two sectors.

Chapter 7 – Blockchain in Manufacturing

Blockchain in the Manufacturing Supply Chain

The manufacturing sector is an essential driver of the world economy. As per a report of the World Bank, this sector has a share of around 18% of world GDP. Sadly, this sector has been rampant with problems in quality control and inefficiency since the Industrial Revolution. With time, the manufacturing industry has increased in demand and volume, and the supply chain has become more complex.

Due to the lack of a process to track the real products, fake products can quickly enter the market. A report of the International Trademark Association puts counterfeit goods at around half trillion an annum. Supply chains are unreasonably disconnected and complex. Therefore, it is not as simple to track as it should be.

Ongoing problems from poor quality to counterfeit and inefficient processes in the manufacturing sector reminds us that we are living in the 20th century, not in the 21st. Blockchain technology can sort out a large number of issues in the manufacturing supply chain.

With the implementation of a blockchain based solution, manufacturers can have control over intellectual properties. The use of a blockchain platform can enable the manufacturers to have a smarter supply chain and to monitor material movements, payments and contracts. It can provide distributed models to the manufacturers, allowing them to make the entire business operation smoother.

Challenges in the manufacturing sector

Some common factors like too long lead times, conventionally low volumes, and global shifts in product requirements define the nature of the manufacturing industry. Besides, the complexity of the manufacturing supply chain (due to the involvement of specific processes) has increased.

In the current world manufacturers are using SCM (Supply Chain Management) solution to maintain the flow of raw materials and produced products. Any challenge to the flow of the supply chain can cause many critical disorders. Here are some of the significant problems of the manufacturing supply chain:

- Globalisation
- Fast-changing market conditions
- Demand variability
- Extended response times
- Quality issues
- Regulatory compliance
- Risk and security
- Transparency in the supply chain
- Lack of collaboration between partners
- Reliability of services
- Technology advancements
- Anticipating purchase and production needs

How can blockchain help manufacturers to face their supply chain challenges?
Like several other sectors, the apparent health of the manufacturing industry is not essentially projecting extraordinary success in the future unless it resolves almost every challenge. The manufacturing supply chain is getting more complicated due to the economic globalisation, increasing expenses and the processes involved.

Here every challenge is explained with practical examples of companies solving the same. It can help to comprehend how a blockchain based solution can help this sector to face its challenges.

Continuous information sharing

At present most of the manufacturers face challenges in having the right information at the right time and sharing the same with their stakeholders and consumers. It causes them having to delay material procurement, product delivery and other allied operations.

With the implementation of a blockchain based solution, manufacturers can have a single platform to access critical information and share the same with all stakeholders and customers. As a distributed platform it allows the stakeholders in the manufacturing supply chain to have continuous information access, and this accelerates the processes involved.

Supply chain auditing/management

As per a survey around 80% of managers of the supply chain have worries about the disruptions in the supply chain. The anxiety is very high in the manufacturing sector as its dependency on materials increases with the rise in product production. Manufacturers are on edge as their dependence on materials have increased the risks of fraud and chain waste from 25.2% to 35% between 2014 and 2017.

To control uneasiness and minimise disruption in the supply chain, manufacturers have started to invest in blockchain to find the right solution. A recent survey states that around 60% of primary manufacturers will be contingent on digital platforms by 2020. These platforms will be liable to support functions that are openly accountable for 30% revenue. The range of new technologies will be implemented in the manufacturing industry. Around 20% of the big players of this industry will depend on the combination of blockchain, IoT, cognitive systems and AI by 2021.

At present trust plays a significant role in the manufacturing supply chain. Implementing a blockchain based solution can change this by making it more enhanced. Manufacturers are working on systems that could help them bring all participants onto a platform, and the participants could update the records at their end at any time.

Skuchain is a company that is working on the use of *smart contracts*, or *Brackets,* to help manufacturers in enhancing transparency in their supply chain.

Lowering barriers for small manufacturers
With time and government support, many startups are entering into the manufacturing sector. As startup companies, they have to face many challenges from producing high-quality products to sustaining in the market. With a limited budget they find it hard to take big decisions such as what to do to find a place in the market.

Blockchain provides solutions to such startups. With a little investment a blockchain based solution can help them in their entire business operations from the procurement of materials to the sale of produced products. The technology helps in having a close look at the whole process.

Information accessibility
At present manufacturers and stockholders of this industry face problems in accessing respective information at their end. Due to this they face difficulty in having the right information on material procurement, product quality and allied business operations.

With the integration of a blockchain based solution, the manufacturers along with all the stockholders have a common platform. By using their private keys they can access the relevant information at any time from anywhere. Accessing relevant information helps them take the required action to make the process smooth.

Reduction in loss due to data breaches

Due to data breaches on its supply chain the manufacturing industry has to face losses. As per a report, approximately 39% of the manufacturers face a loss of 1–10 million US dollars each year. The hacked data relates to individual credentials and intellectual property.

Implementing a blockchain based solution can help manufacturers stay protected from all types of data hacking. As a distributed ledger it requires the permission of all stakeholders in a single platform to validate data entry and the changes made to the system. Having many parties in a single distributed platform makes it impossible for hackers to have full access to the system. A blockchain network enables the manufacturing industry to have constant communication with all its stakeholders, and this prevents fraud that can cause minor to significant system failures.

Trust enhancement in products via public data

With time hackers became more active and sophisticated. It caused a significant rise in the fraud cost to 3.7 trillion US dollars in the manufacturing sector. Corruption is also an issue that around half of the manufacturers face in their supply chain, logistics, product productions and material procurement.

In the manufacturing and shipment of food products, fraud is seriously dangerous. It can cause some serious issues with health. Further, it can even lead a person to death. In America there are around 70% fraud and corruption, while China is closer to a 100 per cent figure in this regard.

Manufacturers have to go through certification processes, and there is no way/system for consumers to get such information. With the implementation of blockchain, the manufacturers can share such information with their customers. Moreover, the customers or any unauthorised person cannot alter the data. This information can also be accessed by the stakeholders of the manufacturing supply chain. As a result, manufacturers can enhance their credibility as ethical and reliable suppliers of goods. Also, manufacturers can have stronger consumer loyalty in return.

IBM & Maersk Partnership is working on to enhance transparency and provenance in the manufacturing supply chain.
Provenance Project is developing a more transparent system by using blockchain.

Better tracking of maintenance
The manufacturing industry finds it hard to calculate downtime cost. A recent survey reveals that more than 80% of the manufacturers find it hard to estimate their real/true downtime cost. Downtime usually occurs due to maintenance issues.

In reality unplanned downtime in a specific category is costlier in comparison to an anticipated one. An Aberdeen research report states that around 82% of manufacturers faced unplanned downtime in the last three years and it cost them about 260 thousand US dollars per hour. For manufacturers dependent on older equipment, the interruption due to maintenance work can be more costly and frequent. For a manufacturer the difference in maintenance cost can be around 100% if it had unplanned downtimes between its two production plants at the same time.

The use of blockchain offers a unique, single source ledger and enables all stakeholders on a supply chain to have real time updated information. Suppose that a person orders a pizza. Domino's keeps the person informed with real time updates on his/her order's status. Applying this concept can help the manufacturing sector escape from unplanned downtime and monitor the progress for ongoing maintenance works.

Securing valuable data
The manufacturing sector has a more significant proportion of fraud than any other industry. This industry has 23% of fraud cases particularly in procurement, and the problem is getting worse day by day. Such a fraud in the manufacturing supply chain takes place due to inadequate record keeping systems, lack of a unique oversight and other flaws. It causes minor to intensive loses to manufacturers and supply chain stakeholders.

Integrating a blockchain based solution can help the manufacturing supply chain to build an absolute and tamper-proof record for all the stakeholders. It can enable this sector to have considerable savings.

Leading manufacturers using Blockchain
By observing the success of blockchain technology in the financial sector, many manufacturers across the world have implemented this emerging technology while several others are working on what such technology can do for securing and enhancing their business operations. Here are some leading manufacturers that have implemented or are working to adopt a blockchain platform:

Apple (America)
This giant computer and mobile manufacturer has got a patent to use this emerging technology to timestamp data.

Ford Motor Company (America)
This giant auto manufacturer has launched a blockchain research centre and obtained a patent to work on how to control traffic flow.

*Nestle (*Switzerland)
This giant food processor/manufacturer is a part of a consortium and is working with IBM to eliminate the unnecessary intermediaries in its supply chain.

Daimler AG (Maker of Mercedez Benz, Germany)
This giant car manufacturer has started to create its cryptocurrency using the Ethereum blockchain.

Samsung (South Korea)
This electronics giant launched its Nexledger platform using blockchain to track its supply chains across the globe.

Toyota Motor Corporation (Japan)
It is a founding member of blockchain Mobility Consortium. This auto manufacturing giant is exploring how blockchain payments can enable self-driving cars.

FedEx
This giant cargo handler is now the first and foremost shipping company to implement a blockchain technology in its management of supply chains. At present the company is using blockchain to track high-value cargo, and it is intended to extend the usage of this technology in its entire business operation.

Maersk
This shipping giant tested blockchain in March 2017 to find out how this technology could help it to manage its cargo. It has collaborated with IBM and is working on how to make its supply chain more transparent, tamper-proof and smooth.

UPS
It joined BiTA (Blockchain in Trucking Alliance) in November 2017 with a hope to bring enhanced transparency among all stakeholders engaged in its supply chain. It is working to build blockchain standards for its freight industry. Besides, it is working on how to utilise blockchain in its customs brokerage business.

In brief, the incorporation of blockchain can help the manufacturing supply chain to eliminate its hurdles and enhance profit earnings.

Chapter 8 - Blockchain in Pharma and Retail

Blockchain in Pharma and Retail

As a distributed ledger blockchain has helped the finance sector a lot, and it has revolutionised this industry. The success of a blockchain technology in the financial industry has encouraged many other businesses to invest in it and find out how this technology can help them change the face of their business operation. Besides, they are working to improve their business profits by removing hurdles.

Industries like pharma and retail are also working on how to use a blockchain based solution to enhance their business operations and earn more profits. Here are separate discussions on these two sectors.

Blockchain in Pharma

From the past three–four decades, the pharmaceutical industry has been one of the top performing industries. The whole sector, from manufacturing to clinical trials, to supply and marketing, has been booming. By updating its business operations with the use of the latest technology, the industry has enjoyed high-profit margins. However, this sector has started facing a decline in its profits due to several challenges and growing competition.

At present the sector is facing challenges like inactive chemicals, damage of ingredients in the supply chain, wrong prescription of medicines due to fault in the system, and counterfeit drugs. These challenges have affected the pharmaceutical industry and enforced it to look for an efficient tool/system that can help the industry to get rid of the same. Fortunately, blockchain can help pharmaceutical companies solve some of these challenges.

How Blockchain can help the pharmaceutical industry
Here are ways how blockchain can transform the pharma industry:

Supply chain integrity
The contemporary pharma supply chain is extremely complex. Its complexity is due to the process of changing product ownerships from manufacturers to suppliers including repackagers, distributors and wholesalers before finally reaching consumers. Due to this the sector has to face a considerable loss of revenue each year.

With the use of blockchain in the current supply chain management solution the industry will have a common platform, and all the stakeholders can easily access the required information by using their private keys. The pharmaceutical sector can resolve most of the challenges related to its supply chain.

Validating the authenticity of returned drugs
In the pharma sector manufacturers have to face frequent returns of medicines. For example, some of the wholesalers place excess order to drug manufacturers. They do this due to their poor inventory. As a result they return the unsold drugs to the manufacturers. The proportion of the returned drugs is small, around 2–3 % of the sales. In today's world the volume of unsold drugs is of approximately seven to ten billion US dollars.

Drug manufacturers opt to resell those drugs instead of destroying them. They have legal obligations to verify the authenticity of the medicines before reselling them. Like the Drug Supply Chain Security Act of the USA and the Falsified Medicine Directive (FMD) in Europe, every country has its own drug regulatory body. The drug manufacturers have to follow the set norms of the respective regulatory body in a particular country.

With the integration of a blockchain based system, pharmaceutical manufacturers can avoid themselves from such a repetitive approach while operating their business in different countries across the globe. They can keep a record of serial numbers of drug packages on blockchain. The wholesalers, retailers and consumers can verify the authenticity of a drug packet by logging onto the system built using a blockchain network.

By collaborating with SAP, Merck has developed an app named as SAP Pharma blockchain PoC. It has studied two cases in 2017 and 2018 to make the app more useful.

Prevention of counterfeit drugs and medical devices
The pharmaceutical companies that formulate, ship and supply drugs to the consumers via wholesalers and retailers have a tough time to track their products with all relevant information. Counterfeiters take benefits from this loophole and introduce fake medicines into the system. Such counterfeiting is extended to the manufacturers of medical equipment too. As per a WHO report, approximately 8% of the medical instruments in circulation are fake.

Fake medicines and medical instruments are a significant risk for the healthcare sector. Besides, they cause considerable revenue loss for drug and medical device manufacturers.

In the USA the Drug Supply Chain Security Act came into force in November 2018. It offers an immutable product identifier for every medicine package and a proof of the authenticity for every sold product. A blockchain based solution can allow involved parties to track all the transaction records. With this it will be harder for counterfeiters to introduce fake medical devices and drugs into the market.

Fritz in collaboration with Novartis is working on a domain architect supply chain to prevent the entry of the counterfeit medicines and medical instruments into the market.

Traceability and transparency of consent in clinical trials
Informed patient consent consists of making the patient well aware of every step of the clinical processes along with the probable risks, if any. The clinical trial process along with its revisions needs to be traceable for all stakeholders and apparent for patients. At present the process of informed patient content is challenging to handle satisfactorily.

An FDI report states that approximately 10% of its all monitored trials have some consent collection issues. The issues are an invalid consent document, unapproved forms and missing intellectual review.

The incorporation of blockchain protocols in clinical trials offers consent transparency and traceability. With its reliable mechanism the technology allows storing, tracking and sharing the consent in a secured and publicly proofing way. With bound smart contract, making any change in the clinical trial protocol will require patient approval.

Enhancement of reliability and quality of clinical trial data
At present there is no reliable system to store clinical trial data and share the same with respective persons like doctors, patients and the authority (for example FDA). In the USA the enforcement of the PDUFA (Prescription Drug User Fee Act) in 1992 allowed the FDA to raise funds from pharma manufacturers. With this the FDA earned around 7 billion dollars as user fees and the ongoing rise in income through fundraising made doctors and patients suspicious. Here the problem is the conflict between the authority and physicians along with the patients hired for clinical trials.

As an immutable and decentralised ledger, blockchain can solve this conflict. Incorporating a blockchain based platform can allow the physicians to store the clinical trial data securely and share the same with the respective stakeholders along with authority. It can prevent the alteration of the clinical trial outputs, and this can enhance the reliability of the clinical trial data.

Besides, this technology can be applied to enhance the quality and quantity of patients engaged in clinical trials. Patients can save and control the access of their sensitive medical data using the platform and make the same visible for the recruiters/researchers. It will help the recruiters save time and avoid collecting medical data for clinical trial. Due to being decentralised, the blockchain based platform allows patients to have control over their data, revocation and consent.

Amgen, Pfizer and *Sanofi* are separately working on how to make this technology more profitable and ensure the reliability of clinical trial information.

Blockchain in Retail
With the rise in popularity of cryptocurrency and the use of blockchain based solutions, businesses of different sectors are eager to know how such a platform can benefit them. The retail industry is one of such segments.

At present the sector is booming. The retail industry (offline and online) deals with the business flow that starts with the procurement of products from manufacturers/wholesalers and ends with the delivery/sale of the same to the customers. It is clear here that the retail industry faces challenges in the supply chain, product quality, customer trust, client service and payment options.

How Blockchain can change the face of the retail sector

Some of the retail owners (both online and offline) have adopted or are working on this technology while some are keen to utilise it in the future. To comprehend how a blockchain based solution will help the sector here are some use cases:

Supply chain transparency
In recent years there has been a significant rise in ethical consumerism and interest in knowing the origin of products. Supply chain management has a crucial part in the retail sector. By incorporating a blockchain based solution in the supply chain, retailers will easily track data in regards to the truck location, product temperature and humidity, stages of the delivery process, and so on.

For example, a supermarket is selling a banana cake. A customer can find the data on the source of the product, manufacturing time, particular ingredients and more. In brief, the retail sector will have an improved supply chain, as all stakeholders will upload the relevant data that can't be altered with the consent of all users of this industry.

Walmart has used Hyperledger Fabric developed by IBM for its pork supply chain, and it is expanding the usage of this blockchain based solution to its entire supply chain. This retail giant is working hard to bring complete transparency to increase its trust among consumers.

Customer trust/customer privacy
With the rise in cyberattacks and frauds, people are very conscious in today's world. Most of the time they think a lot before sharing their contact details with retailers. They are afraid of misuse of their shared personal data.

With the integration of a blockchain based platform, retailers can ensure their customers that their secret data is safe with the company. This integration will help the retail players to gain their consumers' trust. To make the data safe and secured, the retailers will give a digital ID to their customers. It will enable their patrons to have faith in them and believe that no one with their consent can change or share their sensitive data.

Loyalty programmes

Blockchain provides the right, instant data integrity. Retailers can take benefit of this feature and use it for their consumer loyalty schemes. With the integration of a blockchain based platform the retail players will ease their data dependency, and they can comfortably use the data for their loyal customers.

Brands like *Coach* and *Tiffany & Co.* can create a loyalty programme which would be interlinked and jointly beneficial. Fortunately, there is a technology *blockchain* which enables retailers with similarly targeted audiences to have a decentralised platform and makes loyalty members liable. It permits customers to accumulate and spend the earned points in more suggestive ways.

Increased payment options

In today's fast world every business values customer convenience. Business owners feel their marketing efforts are worthless if they fail to convince customers to make quick transactions. As per a survey only 1.2 billion people have bank accounts with payment options while more than 5 billion people have mobile phones. The data regarding mobile users can play a crucial role and help retailers facilitate their customers to use mobiles for making payments.

TelCoin, a blockchain based mobile payment company, is collaborating with telecom companies with an aim to offer convenient and secure payment options. This initiative will give a safe payment method and offers an instance of how businesses with similar target customers use a blockchain based platform together.

Crypto incentive

Blockchain fuels decentralisation and it with its distributed ledger has the potential to change the face of current business operations of different sectors. In today's world people want to save on everything they purchase or avail. Besides, they want to get something in return when they refer to a plan/idea to someone.

Retailers can offer incentive programmes to their loyal customers. The retail players will offer crypto-based incentives to the customers for their referrals. Only the downside with the cryptocurrency is volatility of the coins such as bitcoin. For avoiding such a violation retailers can use the WishKinish. Merchants can use this blockchain based solution to optimise the referrals of their patrons. With this the retail players can have no issue in offering crypto incentives, and their customers can continue shopping more comfortably.

Automated customer service

Customers love being served at once when they are looking for particular products/services. They want to get their queries solved as soon as possible. At present retailers have resources to have a close watch on the behaviour of their existing customers. However, they fail to serve their customers in real time. It happens due to any potential fault or no proper use of the available data.

With the adoption of a suitable blockchain based solution, players of the retail industry have the right information at the right time about their customer behaviours. Having a look at the data enables the retailers to serve consumers with the right products/services at the right time. They find it easy to inform their customers with ongoing promotions and discount offers on selected items via SMS, emails, etc. In simple words, retail players have enhanced customer service by integrating a blockchain technology.

Retailers using Blockchain

Alibaba

This e-commerce giant has developed a blockchain based food supply chain and it is going to invest a series of 14 billion American dollars in working on the use of blockchain.

Amazon Inc.

This US based e-commerce giant provides cloud integrations for several blockchains and has collaborated with *ConsenSys*, an Ethereum startup, for doing more works on blockchain.

Walmart

This world-famous retailer is using Hyperledger Fabric on its pork supply chain, and it has extended its usage of blockchain on other supply chains.

Chapter 9 - Blockchain in Social and Media

Blockchain in Social Enterprises and Media
The world of business has evolved with society from ancient time. Now it is changing along with both community and technology. With the use of technology, society is more interlinked than ever before. The internet has revolutionised society and brought people across the globe closer. Besides, it has allowed new businesses to grow and enhance the environmental, social and financial well-being of the world.

The next technology that can impact society is blockchain. Many people relate this technology to cryptocurrency transactions, and the profound impact in the financial sector backs it. This technology, like previous technologies, has the potential to do a lot for society. It can help record any exchange or transaction like voter identification, property sales and proper distribution of funds among the needy. Besides, it can enable compliance regulatory or automated governance. Like the internet used by more than half of the total world population, blockchain can transform the whole society across the globe.

How Blockchain Can Transform Social Enterprises
Several businesses, especially IT, are exploring the potential use of blockchain for society. They are investigating how they can use this emerging technology or a platform based on it for the community. Due to its significant success in finance, no one has doubts about its potential. Several social enterprises are working on the use of this technology through their innovative projects. Having a look at the challenges of society and the enterprises trying to solve the same is enough to comprehend how this technology can change the face of social enterprises.

Unique Identity Management

As per a report of the United Nations one in five people across the globe has no legal identity, and the ratio is higher among refugees. The problem is due to the absence of a proper documentation process and lack of the required documents with that individual.

Based on blockchain, the projects of *Humanised Internet* and the *World Identity Network* can save the relevant data like a birth certificate and educational documents. Users would have complete control over their sensitive data. However, they can allow anyone to access the data anywhere in the world. It will be beneficial for an individual to have an identity at international level, and volunteers can quickly go to help human beings in case of emergency.

Besides, MONI (a startup social enterprise in Finland) has developed a card which is interconnected to a blockchain based unique digital identity. This platform will allow a refugee to shop or make transactions across the world without having any issues.

Reduction in Poverty

Governments all across the world do planning to reduce poverty. For this they come up with various programmes. Still, there has been no significant change in the number of poor. In the current world (21st Century), a large number of people are earning below 50 dollars a month. This income is even lower than the one-fourth of the average salary in the USA and the UK.

It is because the poor have no direct access to those plans offered by the respective governments. With the use of this technology based solution, governments across the globe help the poor to avail the facilities made available for them without any intermediaries. *Consuelo*, a Mexico based company, has discovered a way how to use this decentralised technology to enable people to avail micro-insurance services.

Transparency in society

Transparency is a crucial attribute of this decentralised ledger technology, and it has helped the technology to attain the success it has now. This feature can help society a lot. The technology can work as the foundation for many vital social projects.

Located in California, BitGive Foundation (a startup social enterprise) has launched the BitGive platform. With the application of this platform users can donate bitcoins to charitable purposes and there will be a record of the whole transaction in real time. There will be a reduction in the transfer fee and the amount will go to the actual recipient.

Welfare with Purpose

Unemployment in today's world is a crucial issue. Governments offer funds to enable the unemployed to live their life. The real problem in the existing world is that the fund doesn't reach to the actual one. With the use of a blockchain enabled platform the governments can ensure the fund disbursement to the right candidate.

The *Universal Benefit Funds* is working on to apply smart contracts so that it could enable itself to enhance accuracy while monitoring social welfare support. With the use of blockchain this firm will engineer a positive impact on society.

Sharing Economies

At present there is no proper way of sharing economies. With the success of this innovative technology in several different business fields, experts expect the emergence of Airbnb type businesses. In such a market the owner will integrate smart contracts that enable peer to peer sharing, and he/she will have control over unalterable conditions like a time limit on hired homes for holiday stays and the speed limit on the electric cars bought by taking a loan.

Decentralised Computing Power

The world needs a supercomputing power. People would share their PC's CPU for this requirement.

Projects like *Golem* are working on this concept. With the use of blockchain, Golem is engaged in developing a decentralised supercomputer. This platform would enable businesses to rent higher processing power and to work or compete globally without the instant cost of expensive hardware.

New Tactics for Behaviour Change

By incorporating the IoT and smart contracts, business organisations can build tokenised or incentivised social nudge campaigns, behaviour change and marketing.

Faith Enhancement in Democracy

People of democratic countries have faith in elections. However, the process of democracy is not without its unusual behaviour. Sometimes voters vote for the wrong candidates and the election authority has to announce new election dates due to fixing or other irregularities held. This makes people have doubts about democracy.

With the integration of a blockchain based solution like *Ballotchain*, governments and society across the globe can strengthen their democratic participation and processes. They can facilitate and manage online voting and the participants can be verified at any time. Social enterprises are working on projects like *Follow My Vote* and *Democracy Earth* to enhance society's faith in democracy. As a blockchain based democracy project, *Horizon State* offers decentralised participation and a decision platform. Working as a digital ballot box it protects votes and data related to voters' information. It allows leaders to mention their agenda to their constituencies. *E-vox* is used for local elections in Ukraine.

Change in Fundraising Strategies

In the current world, charity or fundraising is in the black. Both charity institutions and donors do not disclose the amount.

Governments, donors or society can use cryptocurrency for bringing transparency in fundraising or donations. With the use of bitcoin, fundraisers can ask for fractional amounts from prominent donors. Charities can pair donations with smart contracts. One person can donate a certain small amount when he/she makes a purchase.

Increase in Exchange of Renewable Energy

There has been no significant change in renewable energy exchanges. However, the use of a blockchain based platform can revolutionise this sector. The delivery will be possible at the local level with peer to peer transfers. *Powerledger*, a Perth-based social enterprise has made plans and is working on a solar power exchange platform, which will use blockchain technology. This platform allows the owners of solar panels to supply surplus solar energy in their neighbourhood. Apart from *Powerledger*, many social enterprises like *SunExchange* and *WePower* are working to increase in renewable energy exchanges.

Accountability in sharing Knowledge

Blockchain can revolutionise knowledge sharing. It can support in the creation of a decentralised Wikipedia knowledge base which would enable editors to be a stakeholder on the platform. This technology will allow contributors to be more accountable while sharing their knowledge. With the use of this technology editors would earn tokens for their valuable contributions, and hence they would be more liable. In the case of inaccuracy they would lose their tokens and the information will not be made live.

Reduction in Corruption

Corruption is a massive issue in society. People in countries like China and India suffer a lot from it. No work takes place here without a bribe.

Accountability and transparency are two weapons for fighting against corruption. Integrating blockchain in social enterprises and public/private bodies will bring transparency in society. Besides, it can make all the concerned persons/bodies accountable for the work. Every work detail will be uploaded on a blockchain based platform, and anyone without tampering can access the data. With this no one can hide any information on public/society work.

Land Rights
Due to irregularities and a lengthy documentation process, people have to lose ownership of their land or property. With the incorporation of a blockchain based solution, people can secure their ownership of the land/property they have.

Bitland, a social enterprise, is working on a project in Ghana. This project will allow people or a group of persons to survey and record the ownership with the same. The people will have an auditable and permanent record. Besides, Bitland is working with the government to resolve land disputes.

A Boost in Environment Protection
The use of a blockchain based supply chain management will help society to work on environmental protection. Being transparent and tamper-proof, it allows the authority and stakeholders to track products from the field to the table and enables us to know whether the products are organic or not. If the product is natural the concerned stakeholder/authority can cancel the order, and it will be a significant step to safeguard the atmosphere of a place.

Everledger, a startup social enterprise, has saved immutable data on more than 1.5 million diamonds to find out the origin of diamond products and support to have control over the supply of **blood diamonds**. Work is going on to develop a translucent global database on coral reefs. With this scientists will be able to protect coral reefs from harm.

Blockchain in Social Media

Social media (Facebook, Twitter, LinkedIn, Instagram, etc.) is a part of daily life in today's world. It has more users in comparison with the computer (desktop/laptop). As per a recent survey, more than 50% of social media users are active on Facebook.

Social networking sites like Facebook and Twitter are culprits of having data leaks complaints and fake news. Sometimes people find it hard to believe in the information/news they come across on social sites. They have no faith even in real stories. Integrating blockchain can transform the face of social media and enable it to face ongoing challenges.

How Blockchain can change the face of social media

Whether one is a business owner or social media marketer, he/she needs to understand that it will go through a striking shift in the future. Organisations usually build their brands on social sites such as Facebook and Twitter and will soon realise that their time investment on social platforms might have been zero. Blockchain has revolutionised many businesses so that it can do the same with social media. Here are some examples of how a blockchain based solution can transform social media:

Better User Control Mechanism

Social networking sites gather a considerable amount of data. These sites have all relevant data about a post when a user publishes it. Till now, how data is gathered and what is done with the collected information is a mystery. A recent study has disclosed that knowledge is influenced, distributed and even sold. For data breach, Cambridge Analytica is a good example.

With the integration of a blockchain based solution there will be a stop on data manipulation or sale. By incorporating the latest blockchain platform like *Skycoin*, users will have complete control over their posts and information. No one can access their personal information without the users' consent. The users will have direct contact with the third parties and advertisers.

Rise in Interest in Setting Online Identities
As people and businesses face massive problems on social networking sites such as Twitter and Facebook, companies are looking for more powerful and secured platforms on which they enhance their ROI.

Businesses are taking interest in having interactions with customers who have used blockchain to keep their identities. In simple words, blockchain has provided an extra option for owners to socialise their businesses and expand their customer outreach.

Reduction in Fake Content
In recent a few months Facebook has been trying to identify and delete accounts responsible for spreading fake content. The company has to do it due to having received several complaints from various regions across the globe.

With the integration of blockchain in social media, there will be a complete stop on the fake content post. This technology can verify the information/post along with users' identity associated with those false content posts. For example, the oxcart protocol offers a framework to enable developers to create a super-powerful app on which each one can manage and authenticate their own real as well as digital assets. The app can also support in collecting and examining all sorts of data from news to information shared on social networking sites.

Capter 10 - How to get started?

How to get started?

Once we understand the value that blockchain can bring, the next step is to find out how to implement it in your enterprise. Since it is a very new technology, we always recommend doing a proof-of-concept. But before we start a project on blockchain the key questions is how to select the correct project. The correct project selection is the key to a successful proof-of-concept. This chapter will give a framework to selection the correct project and then select a correct platform for selecting the blockchain platform.

Project selection
Selecting a correct project is the first step for a blockchain proof-of-concept. There is a series of questions that we should ask ourselves before we start a PoC. Check the decision tree below:

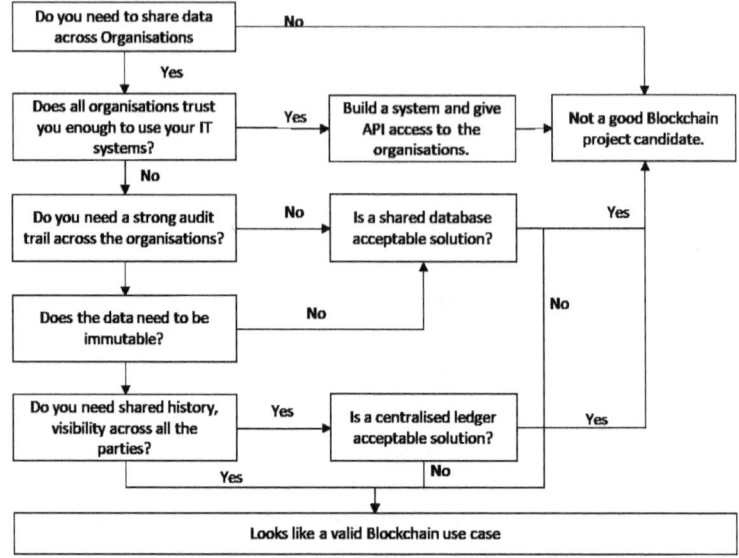

Blockchain Platform Selection:

Once you have selected your use case, the next big decision is to select the platform. For selecting the platform, please use the following factors:

Permissioned vs Permission-less

If you need to have all your participants authorised before participating in the network, then you will need to use the permissioned network. But please remember the permissioned network need to identity verification/authorisations services sometimes known as notaries. These services can be either centralised or decentralised, so check what is suitable for your use case.

Tokens/Crypto or not

If you are looking to create cryptocurrency or want to tokenise an assess on the blockchain, then please remember not all the frameworks provide this functionality. For example, Hyperledger Fabric or Corda DO NOT provide any facility to create token or crypto. If you need an enterprise-ready blockchain platform with Tokenization, your choices are extremely limited.

Developer availability

There are not many developers available in the market on most of these technologies. The problem is even more complicated with the fact that many of these frameworks have their languages created, which makes it even harder to train your existing developer pool.

Speed of transactions

If you are looking for thousands of transactions per second, then your choices are limited to mostly permissioned blockchain. Few permission-less blockchains claim that kind of scalability but are not proven yet.

Granular security

Not all platforms provide the granularity of the security needed in an enterprise IT system. Do look at each of the platforms and review the security granularity.

I hope these factors will provide you a good view of the factors that you will need to consider before your blockchain project.